Arthur C. Grissom

Beaux and Belles

Arthur C. Grissom

Beaux and Belles

ISBN/EAN: 9783743303492

Manufactured in Europe, USA, Canada, Australia, Japa

Cover: Foto ©Thomas Meinert / pixelio.de

Manufactured and distributed by brebook publishing software
(www.brebook.com)

Arthur C. Grissom

Beaux and Belles

Beaux and Belles

By

Arthur Grissom

✽

G. P. PUTNAM'S SONS

NEW YORK   LONDON
27 West 23d St.   24 Bedford St., Strand

The Knickerbocker Press

1896

TO MY SWEETHEART
FRIEND, AND WIFE

PREFACE.*

A certain Bard (as Bards will do)
Dressed up his Poems for Review.

Austin Dobson.

Short is the date, alas, of modern rhymes,
And 't is but just to let them live betimes.

Pope.

* For the privilege of republishing these
verses, special acknowledgment is due to the
editors of *Leslie's Weekly, Life, Truth, Vogue,
Town Topics, Godey's Magazine, Munsey's,
Overland Monthly, Dramatic Mirror, New
York Herald,* and *The Chap-Book.*

▼

CONTENTS.

vii

Contents

Contents

Contents

AT CUPID'S COURT.

1

THE WAIF.

WHITE ladies, proud and great,
   Sweet ladies and most dear,
Bend from your high estate,
  And hear me, ladies, hear ;
A moment stay the dance,
  I, Cupid, at the door,
Beseech you for a glance,
  One tender word implore !

A homeless stranger I,
  An outcast of the storm,
So cold in passing by
  I needs must stop and warm ;
Please drive me not away,
  And do not frown, or scold,
Have pity, ladies, pray,
  I am so cold—so cold !

Once, in a happier time,
  I was a welcome guest

Beaux and Belles

In every home and clime
  With youth and beauty blest ;
And ladies great as you,
  In jeweled silks and lace,
Esteemed me fair and true,
  And blushed to kiss my face.

Ah, those were happy days !
  But all their joys were vain ;
Maids wearied of my ways,
  And gave me cold disdain,
Because, forsooth, there came
  My rival, base and bold,
Who stole their souls.   His name ?
  His name—ah, me !—was *Gold*.

Since then, from sun to sun,
  I 've wandered far and near,
A vagrant maidens shun,
  And flout, and spurn, and fear ;
Yet would I do no harm,
  Kind ladies, this I swear,
More than to teach the charm
  Of living to the fair !

4

At Cupid's Court

Behold, my broken bow,
   My quiver's need of darts ;
I know not where to go
   To find unselfish hearts ;
Please, ladies, bid me stay,
   The snow is cold and high,
Have pity, ladies, pray,
   Have pity, or I die !

PRINCESSE CHARMYNGE.

SHE is Belle of all yᵉ Towne !
   Whenne she Comes & Goes,
How hʳ rivalles frette ande frowne !
What a general bowynge downe
   Of yᵉ Beaux !

She is fayre, & franke, & swete,
   Scarce beyond hʳ teenes ;
But adourers at hʳ feete
Fynde hʳ sovereigntie compleat
   As a queen's.

Whenne she smyles or spekes, yᵉ aire
   Semes to thryll with Songe ;
Yf for one she semes to care
Alle besyde are inne dispaire
   At yᵉ wronge !

Who colde saye wʰ· She will wed ?
   Will he ryches owne ?

At Cupid's Court

Will he, whenne ye vows are sayde,
Askynge for a hearte, instedde
    Get a stone?

Ah, my Secrett will not downe!
  Yett—how can it be?
She, ye beautie of renoune,
She, ye Belle of alle ye Towne,
    Loves but Me!

EVENING IN BROADWAY.

THERE is hurrying up and down,
  There is laughter in Broadway,
For the beauties of the town
  Now are trooping to the play ;
They are come from Murray Hill,
  From the houses tall and fine
By the Park and where you will,
  From their dinners and their wine.

You can mark them as they go
  By their stately swing and dash,
You can hear their laughter low,
  You can see their jewels flash ;
They are robed in silks and furs,
  They have not an earthly care—
Débutantes and dowagers,
  All are happy, all are fair.

And the men who walk beside,
  With their sable cloaks thrown back,

At Cupid's Court

Showing bosoms white and wide
  In relief against the black,
With their boots of fleckless gloss,
  Lofty hats and silvered sticks,
Think no more of gain and loss,
  Games of greed or politics.

There is joy in every breast,
  Hope is sweet when eyes are fond,
Life is now a careless jest,
  And no sorrow lies beyond.
Are there souls in misery?
  Who remembers in his mirth?
In the glow of lights they see
  Naught of all the gloom of earth.

Note the shifting up and down
  Of the pageant in Broadway,
All the beauties of the town
  Trooping gayly to the play!
Will a mimic scene compare
  With their own, do you suppose?
Now they vanish, and the air
  Smells of violet and rose.

THE DÉBUTANTE.

BETWIXT the blooming and the bud,
　　As 'twixt the dawnlight and the day,
She, radiant with youthful blood,
Stands on the verge of womanhood,
　　Seeming to say :

" Behold me ! I am chaste as light !
　　Behold me ! I am very fair—
Yea, I am fair in all men's sight,
A flower no shame or sin may blight,
　　Mocking despair."

I know this, having lived thus long :
　　To human eyes the fairest thing
In all this world of woe and wrong,
Is maidenhood—incarnate song,
　　Symbol of spring.

I know this, learned of all-wise Time :
　　God's masterwork it is ; I know

At Cupid's Court

'T is sweeter, fairer, more sublime,
Than aught else told in rune or rhyme
    Written below.

Believing this, as all men must,
  I marvel at the ill man hath
To be a traitor to her trust,
To poison her sweet lips with lust,
    Knowing God's wrath.

TO AN OLD PORTRAIT.

(BY A MODERN CYNIC.)

GOOD lady, you were once, I 'm told,
 A famous belle, of many graces,
Who won the hearts of young and old,
 And loyal praise in royal places ;
Who danced, coquetted, played, and sung,
 Until your maidenhood departed,
Were wed, but passed away while young,
 And left a hundred broken-hearted !

A nice and proper record—yet
 You 'd nowadays be voted stupid ;
Now really, did you *quite* forget
 To give at least one shock to Cupid ?
Dear me ! how *could* you please the men,
 And make a lasting reputation,
Without o'erstepping, now and then,
 The narrow limits of your station ?

12

At Cupid's Court

That 's why you died so soon, of course,
  'T is often so with those so moral ;
If you had only tried divorce,
  And told the public all the quarrel !
If you had gone upon the stage,
  And sung falsetto in the chorus,
Heigho, but you 'd have been the rage—
  And still would live to plague and bore us !

'T is said that you were true and frank,
  And ne'er indulged in tales misleading,
And never smoked, and never drank,
  Nor suffered ills from over-feeding ;
That when you went about at night,
  To ball or play, where tongues are spiteful,
You kept your chaperon in sight,
  Yet seemed to think your life delightful !

'T is also said you sometimes took
  A friendly interest in your neighbors,
And that—oh, horrors !—you could cook,
  And knew somewhat of household labors ;
That once you sewed a button on
  Your husband's shirt—a servant's duty—
And once you waked and rose at dawn—
  Yet managed to preserve your beauty !

13

Good lady, here I lift my hat
  In meek obeisance to your virtue;
Believe me when I venture that
  Your modesty in nowise hurt you;
You make it plain to me, at last—
  The thought is strange—almost alarming—
A woman not bizarre or fast
  May yet be admirable and charming!

A GENTLEMAN OF THE OLD SCHOOL.

YOU would not think to see him there
　　That he had passed threescore and ten
So straight he stands, so bright his eye—
　　So much more grand than other men !

His courtly mien, his knightly grace,
　　The gallantry he ne'er forgets,
Are so distinguishing you think
　　That he was born with epaulets !

He brings to mind the storied days
　　Of chivalry in feudal lands,
When cavaliers in lace and gold
　　Bent low to kiss their ladies' hands.

One fancies that when Death shall come
　　And pluck his sleeve, with sombre nod,
With hand upon his heart he 'll make
　　A grave obeisance to his God !

VIE DE SOCIÉTÉ.

SHE boasts a crest and coat-of-arms ;
  Her grandsire fought at Bunker Hill ;
By virtue of her wealth and charms
  She rules her gilded world at will ;
Her life is one of fine display,
  Indulgence and extravagance ;
She only lives from day to day
  To dress, and drive, and dine, and dance.

And while she shines at play or ball,
  Or at her own exclusive teas,
Or chats throughout a morning call
  Of courts, *chiffons*, and coquetries,
Her husband, as he goes and comes,
  Sends now and then his best regards,
And finds diversion in his chums,
  His clubs, his cognac, and his cards.

So, like the lilies of the field,
  They toil not, neither do they spin ;

At Cupid's Court

" A bore ! " they say, and yawn, and yield
  To each " smart " folly, fad, and sin.
And what has life for such as these ?
  Not I have envy or regret ;
I have my pipe, my ale and cheese,
  My brush, my garret, and Favette !

WEDDED.

I WAS married last night, my dear fellow—
　　You remember sweet Isabel Wright?
Of course—'t was at old Monticello
　　You brought us together that night.
The waltz was "The Love of a Siren";
　　So trustful and warm was her hand,
I laughed as I quoted from Byron
　　Of "vows that are traced in the sand."

You know how my love was a passion
　　From the moment we met at the ball;
Both favorites of fortune and fashion,
　　We reigned in that glittering hall!
I fancy we caused a commotion,
　　As we swept past the guests of degree,
While she sweetly concurred in my notion
　　That the sirens were all in the sea.

She gave me her promise that season,
　　'Neath the moon, on the sands of the shore;

At Cupid's Court

I loved all the more for the reason
    I had ne'er loved a woman before.
Naught is sweeter than love but requital—
    Gossip called us a well-mated pair—
I was lacking in naught but a title,
    And she was angelically fair.

Yes, married—'t was in sound of the ocean ;
    She was regal, my boy, she was grand ;
I shall never forget my emotion
    As I watched her and thought of the sand.
She posed with the grace of a fairy,
    Like a statue in marble I stood ;—
She was wed to the Marquis Old Harry,
    And I, to my bachelorhood !

MY LADY'S BOUDOIR.

" Cælebs quid agam ? "—HORAT.

A SWEET and subtle, rare perfume,
    That seems to charm the wayward
       sense
    Like some weird witch's strange in-
       cense,
Pervades the silence of the room.

One swift, shy look doth these reveal :
    Much rare old lace from inner France ;
    Some gay mementos of the dance ;
A curious old-time spinning-wheel ;

An ivory curio from Japan ;
    A wingèd god from buried Rome ;
    A sealskin from a Northland home ;
A worn prayer-rug from Ispahan ;

At Cupid's Court

The harp of some quaint Tyrolese ;
   A mandolin from sunny Spain ;
   A seagull, stuffed, that winged the main—
A host of queer things such as these.

Soft cushions, pictures, curtains rare ;
   A couch for which a queen might sigh ;
   All things that please the artist's eye,
And luxury is everywhere.

It seems a glimpse of things above,
   A bit of heaven dropped to earth ;
   A place that might give hallowed birth
To wondrous witcheries of love.

I trespass on forbidden ground,—
   I must discovery beware ;
   When sounds her step upon the stair
I 'll haste away, and not be found.

I steal one look—a shameful sin !
   I feel the danger of delay,
   But when I start to go away,
I hear my lady's voice : "Come in !"

IDEALS.

THEY did not meet in glittering hall,
  At birth and beauty's court,
Nor yet at banquet, play, or ball,
  The scenes of Fashion's sport ;
Nor anywhere among the throng
  Of gilded Folly's slaves,
Whose queens make wealth the cloak of
    wrong,
  Whose kings are secret knaves.

They did not meet among the flowers
  All in a garden fair,
Where birds and bees beguile the hours,
  And love is in the air ;
Where Nature dons her richest robe,
  To charm all eyes that see,
And groups the graces of the globe
  In bowers of Arcady.

At Cupid's Court

They did not meet in foreign climes,
　'Neath cold or sunny skies,
'Mid Scottish hills or Spanish limes,
　Or where sweet Como lies ;
They did not meet in summer, spring,
　In winter, or in fall ;
Ideals are aye evanishing—
　They did not meet at all !

COQUETTE! Above h^r fancie worke
 H^r fancie strayes from lace to lovers,
& who shalle saye what deepe plans lurke
 Withinne h^r hearte, as Cupid hovers
Aneare to aide, with readye bowe,
Inne layinge some new lover lowe?

GRANDMA'S WEDDING GOWN.

L O ! here is grandma, just stepped down
    From the picture on the wall,
Dressed in her famous wedding gown,
    To attend the fancy ball !
No wrinkle mars her dear, sweet face,
    She looks, with cheeks aglow,
Just as she looked, in pearls and lace,
    Seventy years ago !

No wonder she was worshipped then
    In all the country-side !
No wonder hearts were broken when
    She wore this gown, a bride !
And, oh ! to-night she 's just as fair
    As when she wore it so,
With girdled waist and powdered hair,
    Seventy years ago !

The satin, once of spotless white,
    Is yellowed with the years ;

Beaux and Belles

The veil that fell in folds of light
  Is stained, but not with tears ;
For grandma's life was one long May,
  As free from ill and woe
As was her perfect wedding-day,
  Seventy years ago !

To-night, in all her youth and grace,
  For all to praise that see,
The old love-light upon her face,
  She comes to dance with me.
Ah, rose so like the parent flower !
  Full soon our love shall know
The joy that crowned *her* bridal hour,
  Seventy years ago !

A GLIMPSE.

HE spoke of Love as a snow-white dove ;
  And this morn, as I raised mine eyes,
A dove, snow-white, flew by in sight,
  And was lost for aye in the skies !

27

BLASÉ.

HE finds no joyance in a rose
   That graced an hour a fair one's tresses,
He laughs at love, as one who knows
   That maids were only made for dresses ;
He tells you looks are ladies' lies,
   That pledges bore unless they 're broken,
And as for tears and tender sighs,
   They only painful stays betoken.

He lives, he says, an age too late,
   For this one's hero is the farmer,
And seeks relief in slurring fate
   Because not born a knight in armor.
Life nowadays is all a blank,
   Containing not one new sensation ;
And what 's a million in the bank?
   Why, nothing but an aggravation !

Dear ! dear ! I cannot quite agree
   With all he says, because—well, Polly

At Cupid's Court

Is not so great and fine, may be,
  But she makes life seem mighty jolly !
I dare say I 'm a simple wight
  To think her pretty, true, forgiving,
But I retain my appetite,
  And find a real delight in living !

VIVETTE.

I 'M sure I cannot understand
　　Just why I love my love Vivette,
She 's not the least bit great or grand,
　　Like many ladies I have met ;
She 's not o'erwise, and *never* thinks
How great *I* am—the little minx !
And laughs if I dare broach a threat—
She has so many faults—and yet—
And yet—

She 's most provoking now and then,
　　And says I *shall* not call her " pet " ;
Somehow I do it soon again—
　　It is *so* easy to forget !
And all the while I wonder why,
When she is but Vivette, and I
Am—well, am *I*, and I regret
That I have told my love—and yet—
And yet—

30

At Cupid's Court

It is the strangest thing I know
 That I should love this sly Vivette ;
Why, she refused me long ago—
 And she a most pronounced brunette !
Is 't not absurd ?—and when I 've said
None but the fairest blonde I 'd wed ?
And I 'm entangled in her net
More every day ! 'T is wrong—and yet—
And yet—

What shall I do ? I think I 'll say :
 " Good-bye, Vivette—good-bye, Vivette,
Hereafter I 'll remain away,
 And all your little ways forget ! "
She will not care—she 'll only laugh,
" Pray don't be sad on my behalf,"
She 'll say—and then a kiss I 'll get.
I think she 's very bold—and yet—
And yet—

THE PASSING OF THE MODERN MOMUS.

"Momus was the god of raillery and repartee; at the feasts of the gods he played the buffoon. His office was to reprove the faults of the gods, which he did in so sarcastic a manner as to put himself out of favor."—*Dwight's Mythology*.

MIRTH and music now have ceased,
  And we 'll drink a standing toast
To the Momus of our feast
  Who amused and vexed us most.

Lo, our Folly's king is dead,
  And the comedy 's at end ;
Ring the curtain ; bow the head ;
  Friend or foeman now is friend.

Fate provided fittingly
  The *finale*, as it chanced ;
Dancing as he bade us we,
  He was dying while we danced.

At Cupid's Court

Harlequin and sage in one,
　Clown and king, but never knave ;
Yet what noble deed was done ?
　Who will weep above his grave ?

Will the merry host he led
　Honor him as great of men ?
Drain the glass once to the dead !
　Ho ! the dance begins again !

I TAKE you up with reverence,
    Although you 're rather scarred and
      seamy,
And never more will charm the sense
    With strains inspiriting or dreamy ;
Methinks if you were tuned anew,—
    You can't be, so 't is but a fancy—
The only music made by you
    Would be a tender plaint for Nancy !

Long, long you 've lain in gloom and dust,
    But many a memory round you lingers ;
You once were loved, and how you must
    Have thrilled at touch of Nancy's fingers !
She played you as she played with hearts,
    For ah, my lady was capricious,
But though love's wounds have grievous
      smarts,
    I vow her playing was delicious !

At Cupid's Court

I envied you a bit, mayhap,
  Your power to please, and sweet successes,
When you reclined upon her lap,
  Responding to her soft caresses ;
I kept my distance, bashful lout !
  And eyed my buckled shoon dejected,
Until my cousin cut me out—
  A thing I 'd really not expected !

And then, when afterward I learned
  From Nancy's sister's chiding letter,
(The which, I own, I kissed,—and burned),
  That she had really loved *me* better,
I had some trouble in my side
  That puzzled Doctor Sheley greatly ;
It grew so bad when Nancy died,
  I 've never got quite well—till—lately.

Heigho ! my eyes are getting weak ;
  Confound me, I 'm a soft old noddy !
I did n't know the past could speak
  So touchingly of anybody.
Ah, me ! To think her old guitar
  Should turn up here !—a priceless token,
Although defaced by seam and scar,
  And broken, as my heart was broken !

ROMANCE AT TEN.

YOU were the Lady of Kiss-Again,
    And I was the Prince de Grand ;
You of the odious Ogre's den,
    And I of the Beautiful Land ;
You were the maiden divinely fair
    Locked in the castle tower,
While I was the knight who rode by there,
    And caught from your hand a flower.

Do you remember the rescue brave ?—
    My climbing the latticed wall,
With oath that I should the maiden save,
    Or else in my own blood fall ?
And how you were borne, on the old gray
        mare—
    You riding behind, astride—
Away to the regions afar and fair,
    As Lochinvar bore his bride ?

At Cupid's Court

The years have plodded along apace,
  And our paths have led us apart,
But how could I ever forget your face
  When you never returned my heart?
Has twenty forgotten the joys of ten,
  And the way to the Beautiful Land?
Ah, still you 're my Lady of Kiss-Again,
  And I am your Prince de Grand!

A FASHIONABLE GRADUATE.

ROMAUNT OF A SIMPLE WIGHT.

'T IS very sad to read of woe,
   And sad to write of trials and tears,
But ah, my grief will overflow
   Unless to sympathizing ears
I pour it forth—a dismal tale—
   Each word will give your heart a wrench ;
This is the burden of my wail :
   She says her *sweet things* all in French !

For instance, if I question " When ? "
   " *Je suis bien prête*," she murmurs low ;
What can a fellow answer then ?
   How can I say I do not know ?
In language plain and old I speak
   The eager love that naught can quench,
While in a manner most unique,
   She says her sweet things all in French !

38

At Cupid's Court

She loves me, that I know full well,
    I 'd swear it by the Book of Grace,
The fact her tender glances tell
    Whene'er she rests them on my face ;
And once, too, in a *billet doux*
    She wrote it, and the truth to clench
She sweetly signed it " *Tout à vous.*"—
    She says her sweet things *all* in French !

I do not mind when they are writ ;
    I take my French book from the shelf,
And close and hard I study it
    Until I know some French myself ;
But when in passion on my knees,
    Her hand in mine, they make me blench ;
I think I 'd rather have her *sneeze*
    Than say her sweet things all in *French !*

Ah, pity me, who hearts possess
    Of tender sympathy for those
Who weep and wail their sore distress,
    Without cessation of their woes.
I vow I 'll violate the laws
    By suicide, in some low trench ;
Thus end my wasted life, because
    She says her sweet things all in French !

S HE promised me, "No word of mine
    Shall cause your faith in me to dim ";
And then, above her glass of wine,
    I saw her *look* at him.

THE " LUCKY GOWN."

THIS, dear, I call my " lucky gown,"
　　This symphony of pink and white ;
With happy heart I 've got it down
　　To wear when Willy calls to-night.
'T is not so beautiful, I know,
　　As others here, and not so new ;
I wore it first—oh, long ago !
　　But then—the old friends are the true.

Some gowns, you know, however fine,
　　A girl will strangely learn to hate,—
'T is so with several of mine,—
　　They always seem unfortunate ;
While others, it appears, are *blessed*—
　　One 's *sure* to have good times in *them !*
Why, *this* one is worth *all* the rest !
　　I love it—every stitch and hem !

'T was made for Clara's wedding-day ;
　　I was her dearest friend, you see,

And when she threw her bride's bouquet,
  It fell *directly* upon me !
I wore it next to Grace's ball ;
  That was a *very* swell affair ;
I had *such* fun ! And—that 's not all—
  You know I first met Willy there !

I think I 'll wear it just once more
  To-night—there, I must hurry down ;
Who 'll say what Fortune has in store
  When one wears such a *fateful* gown ?
Now, *don't* you think it looks quite well ?
  Oh, my ! I 'm trembling so !—who knows
But Willy, yielding to its spell,
  May feel encouraged to—*propose !*

DEAD in an alien land, and alone !
　　Shot by a bravo, swarth and bold ;—
Dead !　Is it true?—and I loved him so !
　　Though bought by another's gold.

I am ready, Lisette, am I not—almost?
　　And now—my rings and my furs are here?
Ah, yes—there—thanks !　I 'm perfect, you
　　　　say ?—
　　I 'll be down in a moment, dear !

Dead ! he is dead—and I sent him away,
　　And I loved him as only a woman loves !
Dead, and alone !—I 'm coming, dear !—
　　Lisette, will you button my gloves ?

SHE tempted me, because her mouth was
    sweet,
  Because I loved the languor of her eyes ;
She was so fair, so fair, from face to feet,
  How could it be, I ask you, otherwise ?
She tempted me, and through my quick-
    ened blood
  Ran riot all the ardor of my soul,
And o'er my face up-rushed the fiery flood
  That told the secret I could not control.
She smiled to see how surely love betrays ;
She was so wise in all the world's sad ways.

Could you have seen her tender, glorious
    smile,
  And read the pleading language of her
    look,
No more than I would you have guessed
    the guile
  That marred the pages of her heart's
    closed book.

I did not know—I was so blinded then—
  My faith had never known the blight of
    loss ;
I did not know that smiles may murder
    men,
  And that the gold of beauty may be
    dross.
I was the prey with which the tigress plays ;
She was so wise in all the world's sad ways.

What meed of triumph and what joy were
    hers
  She best may tell who saw my pain and
    shame ;
All honor that a love betrayed confers
  Redounded to the greatness of her name.
But in that piteous aftertime when Fate
  Decreed her faith should be as mine de-
    nied,
And chance disclosed her doomed and
    desolate,
  I saw how poor a thing had been her
    pride.
Thus God provides His vengeance and re-
    pays ;
She was so wise in all the world's sad ways.

A LOVE SONG.

GO to, sad fears of love's harsh reign ;
 If love a bondage be,
'T is sweeter far to wear the chain
 Than rule a kingdom free !
Go to, all cold, unreasoning pride ;
 False dignity, away !
The joy is mine for which I sighed,
 And I 'm a slave to-day !

'T is well the hollow creeds of youth
 Have passed away so soon,
'T is well to learn the happy truth
 While life is in its June ;
And when I look into her eyes,
 So fair a world I view,
I know that love has made me wise
 To be forever true !

SHE'S only an "old-fashioned girl," she
    says,
  (Is it not enough to disgrace?)
An "old-fashioned girl" with womanly ways,
  And a winsome and womanly face ;
A girl who is innocent, modest, and sweet,
  Who is sensible, earnest, and true—
The kind that will surely be obsolete
  In another short year or two.

She is n't ambitious for questionable fame,
  She does n't ape man in her dress,
She does n't read books that have a bad name,
  Nor herald her "views" in the press ;
She does n't use slang, nor smoke cigarettes,
  Nor loudly expound "Woman's Rights,"
She shuns all the fads of the "fashionable
    sets,"
  And "home" is her chief of delights.

47

She's only an "old-fashioned girl," you see,
   And not in the least "up-to-date,"
But she is the kind of a girl for me,
   And the kind that I want for a mate.
I know it is very "old-fashioned" to say
   Your wife is a "saint from above,"—
But I own I am fond of her "old-fashioned"
   way,
   And proud of her "old-fashioned" love!

MY LADY OF THE MARIGOLD.

MY Lady of the Marigold is fair to look
    upon,
The fairest queen in all the sunny West ;
Her eyes are like blue violets, all dewy in
    the dawn,
    Her tresses like the marigold that 's pinned
    upon her breast.
She wanders in the garden ; the birds attend
    her there ;
The roses lend their color to her cheeks ;
The sunlight lingers lovingly upon her flow-
    ing hair,
    And all the flowers lean to hear the music
    when she speaks.

My Lady of the Marigold wears neither silks
    nor lace ;
    Upon her wrists there gleam no costly
    bands ;
But knight or king ne'er knelt before a queen
    of gentler grace,

To sue for priceless favors from her white
and jeweled hands.
My Lady's radiant jewels are two bewitching
eyes ;
Her gold she plucked beneath her window-
shrine,
And oh ! the wealth of tenderness that in her
action lies,
When in my hand she places hers, and
lifts her lips to mine !

My Lady of the Marigold, I love you well
and true ;
I ne'er again, O love, will leave your side ;
My world of cold hypocrisy shall not enfetter
you,
But in some far and lovely realm alone we
two shall bide.
We 'll dream beside blue waters, that dance
upon the shore ;
Our ships will be white clouds that sail the
sky ;
The marigolds will bloom for you, the birds
sing evermore,
And all the world—the happy world—will
be just you and I !

TO JULIA.

(IN IMITATION OF HERRICK.)

JULIA ! Since your lips are red
   From the rose that on them bled ;
Since your breath is sweet as wine
Sipped from cups of eglantine ;
Since your mouth, a Cupid's bow,
Seems with blissful love aglow—
Tempting, as a mouth should be—
Guess I 'll take a kiss or three !

HOW very strange! This fan was white,
    When on it I began to write,
But lo! it blushed a rosy red
On hearing what I—might have said!

BALLADE OF SPRING DEPARTURE.

FAREWELL to Town—the Season's done;
   Farewell to banquet, ball, and play,
Farewell to folly and to fun,
   And all that made the Season gay !
   The time has come to hie away
Beyond the pale of Fashion's throng,
   Our steamer leaves at break o' day—
We 're going to do the Contin*ong* !

'T is not good form for anyone
   Who aims to be of vogue *au fait*,
And with the swagger set to run,
   At home or club to longer stay,
   So close the blinds without delay,
And let us pack and haste along ;
   With vast importance and display
We 're going to do the Contin*ong* !

Our tour at Havre will be begun,
   We'll be at Buda-Pesth in May,

Beaux and Belles

At Berne we 'll view the rising sun,
   In Rome the old Flaminian Way ;
   Beside the Rhine we mean to stray
A fortnight—which we *may* prolong ;
   Let all the Papers know, we pray,
We 're going to do the Contin*ong* !

Servants, now don't the truth betray,
   For that would be exceeding wrong ;
Though bound for Jersey, still we *say*
   We 're going to do the Contin*ong* !

SOME poets sing of sweethearts dead,
  Some sing of true loves far away,
Some sing of those that others wed,
  And some of idols turned to clay ;
  I sing a pensive roundelay
To sweethearts of a doubtful lot,
  The passions vanished in a day—
The little loves that I 've forgot.

For, as the happy years have sped,
  And golden dreams have changed to gray,
How oft the flame of love was fed
  By glance, or smile, from Maud or May,
  When wayward Cupid was at play ;
Mere fancies, formed of who knows what ?
  But still my debt I ne'er can pay
The little loves that I 've forgot.

O joyous hours forever fled !
  O sudden hopes that would not stay !

Held only by the slender thread
  Of memory that's all astray.
  Their very names I cannot say,
Time's will is done ; I know them not ;
  But blessings on them all, I pray—
The little loves that I 've forgot.

L'ENVOI.

Sweetheart, why foolish fears betray?
  Ours is the one true lovers' knot ;
Note well the burden of my lay—
  The little loves that I 've *forgot.*

A FAN FANCY.

(Rondeau.)

UPON her fan where Cupids play
  At blind-man's buff in droll array,
 A bit of rhyme he dares to write
 Whose theme is Love, and Love's delight ;
Oh, bold, bad man ; what will she say?

And while she reads he looks away,
To awkward doubts and fears a prey ;
  "Oh fool !" he thinks, " to love indite
    Upon her fan !"

He starts to go ; she bids him stay,
Then blushes, sighs, and—names the day !
  Ah, clever maid ! ah, happy wight !
  Behold a couple's lives made bright
By just a couplet light and gay
    Upon her fan !

AT THE BAL MASQUÉ.

BEHIND her mask two dancing eyes
  Glance up at me in shy surprise
That I, who love her, should presume
To clasp her in the brilliant room,
Where sounds of mirth and music rise,
And claim her as my own fair prize;
True love is fooled by no disguise!
  I caught her smile, her lips' perfume
          Behind her mask!

As well, true love hath enterprise,
Else, Prince (who on all lovers spies),
  How come we in this bower of bloom,
  Where, all unnoticed in the gloom,
I steal a kiss from lips love-wise,
          Behind her mask?

DALLIANCE.

(Triolet.)

I THOUGHT to write an epic grand,
  Instead I turned a triolet ;
With the old masters close at hand,
I thought to write an epic grand ;
A flaming rose was in demand,
  But pleased, I plucked a violet.
I thought to write an epic grand,
  Instead I turned a triolet.

SOUVENIR DE JEUNESSE.

I CAUGHT a rosebud from her hair,
   She bent her head in sweet assent;
Trembling—she was so wondrous fair—
I caught a rosebud from her hair;
How kind she was on that dim stair!
   While asking for the love it meant
I caught a rosebud from her hair.
   She bent her head in sweet assent.

SHE loves not me, forsooth,
   It is only Love she loves ;
Ah, yes, it is all the truth—
She loves not me, forsooth,
Only my strength and youth,
   My presents of gowns and gloves ;
She loves not me, forsooth,
   It is only Love she loves.

WITH HER RED LIPS SO LIKE THE ROSE.

WITH her red lips so like the rose,
    (I kiss the rose's petal tips)
And she so tempting near, who knows,
With her red lips so like the rose,
But by mistake (she must suppose
    It so), I kiss instead her lips !
With her red lips so like the rose,
    Why kiss the rose's petal tips?

SONGS IN SEASON.

63

A SPRING SONG.

OH, Peg is a winsome lassie,
　　And Peg is gentle and shy,
And Peg has the sun in her ringlets
　　And the blue of the sea in her eye.
I found her down in the meadow,
　　On a morn when the spring was young,
And I kissed her lips a score of times,
　　And this is the song we sung :

Ohone ! but it 's time to be merry ;
　　O hey ! but it 's now to be glad ;
For I 'm in love with my lassie,
　　And she 's in love with her lad !

And the day it was fair and balmy,
　　As the days that the poets sing,
And we found the path through the woodland
　　By the old forgotten spring,
Where once before in the summer
　　That passed away too soon,

Beaux and Belles

We gathered the yellow jonquils,
  And sang this happy tune :

Ohone ! but it's time to be merry ;
  O hey ! but it's now to be glad ;
For I'm in love with my lassie,
  And she's in love with her lad !

And Peg with her shy, sweet dimples,
  Playing hide-and-seek with her smiles,
Gave me her hand for safe-keeping
  As we sat on the meadow stiles ;
And I filled her arms with daisies,
  And I filled her lap with yew,
And all the long way homeward
  We sang of hearts that are true.

Ohone ! but it's time to be merry ;
  O hey ! but it's now to be glad ;
For I'm in love with my lassie,
  And she's in love with her lad !

PRIMAVERA.

LIGHT laughter ringing sweet,
  The sound of dancing feet,
    A burst of song ;
A girl as dear to me
As sunlight to the sea,
From guile and grief as free
    As rose of wrong.

What though the throstle sing,
For very joy of spring,
    With silvery note,
The music that I hear
Is sweeter and more dear
Than e'er charmed mortal ear
    From thrush's throat !

O, hasten, blooms of May !
O, hasten, nuptial day
    And honeymoon !
When to my yearning breast
My loved one shall be pressed,
And love be crowned and blest
    In life's long June ! .

NEW YORK, April 2, 1895.

67

UNDER THE RED LILY.

A SHEAF of Easter lilies lies
   Beneath my dear donzella's head,
And blue as fair Italia's skies,
   Blue iris lilies form her bed,
While, with its crimson lily, flies
   The flag of Florence overhead.

The Easter morn is more than fair,
   And all the land in glory gleams ;
Glad anthems fill and thrill the air
   From birds and bells and singing streams,
And from the white cathedrals where
   The "City of the Lilies" dreams.

This day I know what joy may be,
   As in my loved one's bower I bide,
And lo ! the fairest flower to me
   Of all the flowers of Eastertide,
Is this fair maid of Tuscany,
   This tiger-lily at my side.

THE HAPPY RIVER.

HOW dreamily the swift hours go !
  I lie beside the Happy River,
And watch the vagrant water's flow,
  The pale, sweet lilies nod and quiver—
This day when all the June is fair
  With bonnet blue and vesture vernal,
With roses twining in her hair,
  And in her eyes a peace supernal.

Oh, you who plod the city's streets,
  And give your lives to toil and traffic,
Can never, with the soul of Keats,
  Know pleasure so divine, seraphic,
As I, who dream the hours away,
  Where linnets sing and lilies quiver,
In blushing June's embrace, to-day,
  Upon the banks of Happy River.

The murmuring water soothes and calms
  The soul that erst was tossed by passion ;

Beaux and Belles

Above me tender southern palms
　　Have spread their arms in loving fashion ;
My couch is all of myrtle made,
　　The myosotis blows me kisses,
The linnet, from a frond-façade,
　　Has set in tune my own heart's blisses.

The June is young ; her breast is warm,
　　Her breath with fragrant blooms is laden,
The robe about her vestal form
　　Is sensuous with the sweets of Aidenn ;
And ah, June's lips are red with love,
　　And oh, June's heart is faithless never,
I think God made the stars above
　　To crown my June a queen forever !

Unknowing all of life's despair,
　　Unconscious of the world's distresses,
I here repose, without a care,
　　Enraptured by my June's caresses ;
I am content with what is best,
　　I praise and bless the All-wise Giver,
My world is where my head doth rest
　　Upon the banks of Happy River !

LOVE-NOTES.

I.

WHEN I hear her laugh, I think
    Of the rippling of a brook,
Starred with blooms along its brink.

When into her eyes I look,
    To my charmèd sense arise
    Dreams of tender, sunlit skies.

When she speaks, I hear the note
    That outpours at sudden dawn
From the startled thrush's throat.

When her lips mine rest upon,
    All my senses seem to reel,
    And I know not what I feel.

II.

" IF thou wilt tell me, dear," she said,
    " How many stars there be.

71

I 'll tell thee all the golden thoughts
  I have each night of thee."

"Oh, countless, then, thy thoughts," I said ;
  "Of thee I have but one :
Merge all thy stars in one great star
  And that is mine, the sun."

III.

"O RAVEN, why are you silent?
  And why do you coo, O Dove?"
"Lo, one is sad, and one is glad ;
  For we are the moods of love!"

IV.

IN the deep, still garden close
  She leaned to my kiss,
And hers the sweet shame of the rose
  That crimsons in bliss,

When the Great Prince comes in his gold
  From gardens above,
And the dewy, flushed petals unfold
  In fulness of love.

" Dear, thou art the white rose," I said,
  " And Love is the sun ;
Is not the rose happiest red?
  Love's will be done."

v.

OH, June is a sweet, red rose,
  With love on its petal tips,
And June has grace and a rare, fair face,
  And a kiss on her fragrant lips.

The buds have burst with their joy,
  The dumb stars dance their delight,
For I love my June, and our honeymoon
  Shall last fore'er and a night !

UNDER A SUNSHADE.

E YES that are languid and dreamy,
  Lips that are temptingly red,
Cheeks that are dimpled and creamy,
  And tresses silken of thread—
(Mine is the chief of disgraces,
  Loving the vision I view !)
Ah, 't is the fairest of faces
  Under this shade of *écru !*

Blossoms that breathe of a bridal,
  Born of the redolent night,
Wafted of winds to my idol,
  Just for her dainty delight.
(What if I yield to temptation ?
  Who could resist it ? Could you ?)
Ah, what an artist's creation
  Under this shade of *écru !*

Truly a model to measure,
  Fashioned by angels above,

74

Songs in Season

Truly a poem of pleasure,
   Aye, and a lyric of love !
(Never a time like the present—
   No one will see if I do—)
Kissing 's exceedingly pleasant
   Under a shade of *écru* !

COACHING.

THE musical trumpet's blast,—
  The sound of laughter gay,—
Then word to start is passed,
  And the tally-ho rolls away.

Out of the city's street,
  Far from the noisy throng,
Into the country sweet,
  It rumbles gayly along.

Over the cool green hills,
  And down through the wooded dales,
Fragrant with daffodils,
  And vocal with calling quails.

Happy each youthful face,
  Merry the mirthful wits,
And lo ! in the footman's place,
  Trumpeter Cupid sits !

ABOARD THE "BUMBLE BEE."

N OW, sailor, spread your fleecy sails,
  And steer for the open sea ;
There 's never a boat this day afloat,
  As fair as the *Bumble Bee !*
And Marjorie, fair Marjorie,
  Stands laughing at my side,
Her blue eyes bright for pure delight
  As over the waves we glide !

To-day we bid good-by to care,
  And leave the world behind ;
On such a yacht it matters not
  If never a port we find !
For Marjorie, fair Marjorie,
  Has pledged her heart to me,
And where we go, why care to know,
  This glorious day at sea !

Then, sailor, hoist the spinnaker,
  And every stitch of sail,

Beaux and Belles

And with a song we 'll fly along,
And kiss above the rail ;
For Marjorie, fair Marjorie,
This day was wed to me,
And so no drone of a chaperon
Is aboard the *Bumble Bee !*

PRESSING AUTUMN LEAVES.

THE sumac glows a brilliant red
　　By tossing plumes of golden-rod ;
The painted frondage overhead
　　Is fluttering downward to the sod ;
Last night there was a frost ; to-day
　　The world is full of loveliness
As through the woodland aisles we stray,
　　Gathering leaves to press.

We loiter gaily up and down,
　　At every step we find a prize ;
" Here's one," I say, " of deepest brown,
　　To match the velvet of your eyes ;
Here 's one of gold, to match your hair,
　　And here is one of scarlet hue
To match your lips——" She cries : " Take
　　　　care !
　　Base flatterer, you !"

79

Beaux and Belles

I like the work of pressing leaves
  With one so fair as Rosalie ;
What fine suggestions one receives !
  The which are acted on by me.
I cannot tell just what occurs,
  For that, dear me ! would not be best,
But you can take my word—and hers—
  More than the leaves are pressed !

THE ARCHERY MATCH.

SHE fits the arrow to its place,
　　She bends the bow with skill and grace,
　The feathered shaft lets fly ;
A look of triumph lights her face,—
　The score 's a tie !

Dan Cupid, who 's a bowman true,
Then boldly tries what he can do
　To bind the tie fore'er ;
Result : the world declares the two
　A well-matched pair !

BOHEMIA AND BOHEA.

THE witch who brewed with cunning art
　　Some draught of love above a flame,
And chanted runes to charm the heart
　　Of false gallant or fickle dame,
Had not the wondrous power, I vow,
　　Of magic and of sorcery
Possessed by her who charms me now—
　　The little witch who brews me tea !

'Mid cushions made of eider-down,
　　With all the busy world afar,
I watch her, in her pretty gown,
　　Bend smiling o'er the samovar ;
No incantation it receives,
　　Her words have naught of mystery,
But what a blissful spell she weaves—
　　The little witch who brews me tea !

Ye gods that drank of nectar bright,
　　Come down and have a cup or two,

I think you 'll find the flavor right—
    'T will seem like good old times to you !
However happy up above,
    Try once Bohemia with me ;
But I reserve the right to love
    The little witch who brews me tea !

Hallowe'en.

A LOVERS' QUARREL.

(Sonnet.)

Scene : The Library. Time : Christmas Eve

GUY (*entreatingly*) :
And are you angry still, my sweet Marie?
MARIE (*coldly*) :
Miss Marston, if you please—do not forget.
GUY (*bitterly*) :
'T were better far if we had never met !
MARIE (*cuttingly*) :
Quite true ;—we need not meet again, need
we ?
GUY (*striding up and down*) :
I wish that Lovelace girl was lost at sea !
MARIE (*sarcastically*) :
How cruel, when last evening she was
" *Pet !* "
GUY (*turning toward her*) :
I did not mean it, dear—I much regret—

MARIE (*moving away*) :

Shall you attend our church's Christmas tree ?

GUY (*suddenly*) :

Who hung that green upon the chandelier ?

MARIE (*defiantly*) :

I did, but be assured I'll not go near !

GUY (*approaching*) :

Why, you are now—I warn you that—

MARIE (*holding her ground*) :

        Good-by !

GUY (*exultingly*) :

Oh, no, sweet ! you must pay——

MARIE (*faintly*) :

      How *dare* you ?—*Guy !*

(*Twenty minutes later*) :

You dear old stupid !—thought I did not know

That I was standing 'neath the mistletoe !

THE SLEIGH RIDE.

WHEN all the world is robed in white
        And merry night
By moon and stars is rendered bright,

And everywhere the sleighing bell
        Rings out to tell
The tale that lovers love so well,

With joy I capture pretty Flo,
        And off we go
Across the glittering fields of snow,

Our sleigh just large enough for two
        Who want to woo,
And keep unfrozen while they do.

I place my arm, in comic haste,
        About her waist,
And find her lips just to my taste.

She shows no traces of alarm,
        For what 's the harm ?
Thus on we speed past cot and farm.

86

Songs in Season

How swiftly now the moments fly !
    The miles go by,
We notice not the darkening sky.

Heigho ! what now ? 'Mid laugh and shout
    We 're tumbled out,
The snow *is* cool, beyond a doubt !

We climb again into the sleigh,
    Then in dismay .
We quickly learn we 've lost our way !

Yes, lost our way ; alas, alack,
    We can't go back—
Down comes a storm upon our track !

In yonder cottage shines a light—
    It 's hardly right,
But there we 'll have to spend the night.

And who should answer at the door
    But Parson Bore,
Who 's oft seen runaways before.

And—well, I don't know what is said,
    But all turn red,
And Flo and I, we—just get wed !

SKATING SONG.

As swift and light as a bird in flight
　　She skims o'er the glistening lake,
And her skates keep time in a merry chime
　　To the music her red lips make ;
Stray snowflakes fly from the frosty sky,
　　Caressing her cheeks and hair ;
While sweet and strong in a skating song
　　Her voice rings on the air :

　　　　Glow, moon, glow,
　　　　　And twinkle, stars, on high ;
　　　　Blow, winds, blow,
　　　　　As over the ice we fly !
　　　　Blow high—blow low—
　　　　　No lass is cold with a lover bold,
　　　　　Heigho !　Heigho !

With a swinging stride I gain her side,
　　And gather her hand in mine ;

And I shout aloud to the jocund crowd
 A challenge they can't decline.
Hurrah for the race ! We set the pace,
 With never a slip or fall,
And a click and a clash as our runners flash
 Far in advance of all !

Hurrah ! Well done ! The race is won !
 No further the need for haste ;
Then her roguish glance betrays the chance,
 And my arm steals round her waist.
Oh, such the delight of a winter's night,
 When the course is clear and long ;
And the skates keep time in a merry chime
 To the rollicking skating song :

> *Glow, moon, glow,*
> *And twinkle, stars, on high ;*
> *Blow, winds, blow,*
> *As over the ice we fly !*
> *Blow high—blow low—*
> *No lass is cold with a lover bold,*
>   *Heigho ! Heigho !*

FOR VALENTINE.

WHAT shall he send for valentine?
    A rose, a verse entitled " Mine "—
A song of love, a bleeding heart,
Pierced by a deadly Cupid's dart—
A fan of rare old lace from France,
Like La Vallière used in the dance—
A dainty ivory miniature
Of Louis Quinze or Pompadour—
A gemmed aigrette that she may wear
To crown the splendor of her hair—
A buckle, filigreed and chased,
To clasp the belt about her waist—
A *bonbonnière*—a case for cards—
A book inscribed " With best regards "—
Which best would please the maid divine?
What shall he send for valentine?

If best the maiden he would please,
He should, perhaps, send all of these ;
But no !   He 'll send (his purse is flat)
A kiss, and let it go at that !

HEIRLOOMS.

THIS ivory casket, jewel set,
    That grandma cherished to the last
In satin sweet with mignonette,
    Contains the treasures of her past.
She was a famous belle when young—
    For she herself has told me so—
And when her wedding chimes were rung
    Full many a heart was wrung with woe.

I lift the lid and scan them o'er—
    Dear souvenirs !—with reverent gaze ;
It is like opening the door
    Of grandma's heart in other days.
If each could tell its own sweet tale !
    But all are silent now as she,
And darkness shrouds the narrow vale
    'Twixt memory and mystery.

Here is the chain that round her throat
    Was fastened at the king's command ;

Here is the letter grandpa wrote
  When he besought her for her hand;
Here is the locket, pierced, that chanced
  To save him from a British gun,
And here a glove, worn when she danced
  The minuet with Washington.

I know no more; I only know
  She loved each one as some old friend,
And that, because she willed it so,
  I, too, shall guard them to the end.
She gave no gold to mine or me,
  But left, instead, a heavy debt
Of love, that keeps her memory
  As fragrant as the mignonette.

February 22.

IVORY MINIATURES.

(SONNETS.)

IF Karl Huth wrought of old with greater
    grace,
  Or with a skill more marvelous and rare,
  'T was not because inspired by one more
    fair,
Or one of more divinity of face.
Some cunning master hand that thrilled to
    trace
  The beauty of Dubarry and Vallière,
  When Watteau reigned, and France had
    not a care,
By this may well have won immortal place.

Within its dainty frame of *fleur-de-lys*,
  The crossed white lilies of the Bourbon
    lance,
It seems to speak, with dreaming eyes, to me
  Of all the vanished glories of romance,
Of days when kings held court beneath a
    tree,
  And nights when Love was conqueror of
    France !

LIKE pure white rose-leaves are her cheeks
    in hue ;
  Of snowy velvet is her sumptuous gown,
  Lace garnitured and edged with eider-
    down ;
Upon her throat pearls gleam like sun-kissed
    dew ;
Her ermine cloak half hides a white suède
    shoe,
  While valley lilies and white violets crown
  The splendor of her beauty, whose re-
    nown
Is great as that which Titian's models knew.

As slowly she descends the marble stair,
  A radiant vision in the brilliant light,
    She looks like some white statue fraught
    with breath ;
And I, who marvel she can be so fair,
  Know that her vestal soul is just as white,
  And that she will be faithful unto death.

A QUAINT old jar of flowered cloisonné,
    That cost a fortune in Satsuma's mart,
And long and patient vassalage to art,
Has graced her mantel, lo, this many a day.
And since that rapturous night long passed
    away
    When first she played the débutante's shy
    part,
    The roses she has worn above her heart
Have found repose within this lacquered
    clay.

O fragrance of unnumbered happy nights !
    What memories of conquest you recall,
Of merry throngs, of music and of lights,
    Of smiles and whispered vows when love
    was all !
Ah, faded petals of her heart's delights,
    Dropped one by one since that first perfect
    ball !

A S snowy white and cold as edelweiss,
  That blooms in solitude on Alpine
    steeps,
  Or in the solemn Schwarzwald's silent
    deeps,
She looks, in truth, like some fair flower of
    ice,
As to the altar of her sacrifice
  The measure of the melody she keeps,
  Impassive, while her rebel spirit weeps
Like some lost soul barred out of Paradise.

Then as she hears the sacred service read,
  " Whom God hath joined . . " the
    mockery of it all
  Brings to her lips a smile of utter woe ;
She dreams this is her funeral day instead,
  And that her bridal raiment is a pall ;
  The envious world applauds, and does
    not know.

SPRING IN TUSCANY.

THE hills are sown with stars of cyclamen,
   And dew-gemmed cups of wild anem-
      ones,
   And near and far the gold acacia bees
Drone drowsy answer to the lark and wren,
And to the happy songs of maids and men,
   While through the laurel and the myrtle
      trees
   Gleam dreamy vistas of blue, sun-kissed
      seas,
And all the Land of Love is glad again.

Like Virgil, chanting strophes to the skies,
   In pillowed ease on blooms of asphodel,
   Beneath the lattice of a bowered tourelle
I lie content, and feast my happy eyes ;
Ah, surely, surely, this is Paradise !   .   .   .
   Yet where is Dante, and where Raffaelle ?

THE ARTIST.

H E wrought with patience long and weary
    years
    Upon his masterpiece, entitled "Fate,"
    And dreamed sweet dreams, the while his
        crust he ate,
And gave his work his soul, his strength, and
    tears.

His task complete at last, he had no fears
    The world would not pronounce his genius
        great,
    But poor, unknown—pray, what could *he*
        create ?
The mad world laughed, and gave not praise,
    but jeers.

Impelled to ask wherein his work was wrong,
    He sought, despairing, one whose art was
        dead,

But on whose brow were wreathed the
bays of Fame ;
The master gazed upon the picture long ;
" It lacks one thing to make it great," he
said,
And signed the canvas with his own great
name !

IDENTIFIED.

A SLEEPING sylphid one fair day I found
   In Daphne's fragrant bowers (the Poet
      saith),
Most strangely like my own Elizabeth,
And with her hair in wreaths of roses bound.

So tranquil her repose, so sweet, profound,
   But for the soft susurrus of her breath,
   I should have deemed such perfect peace
      was death,
And flung myself, despairing, to the ground.

So strangely like my own sweet love was she,
   I bent and kissed her red lips o'er and o'er,
As flowers are sipped of honey by the bee,
   And spoke the name of her I most adore ;
She oped her eyes, and smiling up at me,
   Exclaimed in rapture : " Please do that
      some more ! "

IN SEVILLE.

THE earth is bathed in fragrance of the
    moon,
  Seville is drunken with the sweets of sleep,
  But one, a pretty youth, doth vigil keep
Beside love's lattice with guitar in tune.

He sings a strain, melodious and sweet,
  To wake his love, who comes with greetings
    warm,
  A pale mantilla round her queenly form,
And broidered brodequins upon her feet.

Her lips meet his in breathless, swift caress ;
  They see not jealous, gleaming eyes that
    peer
  From out the shadows of the cypress near,
Nor hear the oath two savage lips express ;
But when at morn she seeks the scented
    shade,
She finds him prostrate, in his breast a
    blade !

THE BALLET DANCER.

(BY A JOHNNY.)

LITHE-LIMBED and lissome and all
    lovely she,
  Swift-footed as a gleam of glancing light,
  Bare-bosomed, and with glittering gems
    bedight,
And garbed in snowy gauze to shapely knee,
She sweeps and swings to luring melody,
  In graceful pirouettes of dazzling white,
  While I—cannot believe her human quite,
And lean and look, and marvel as I see.

O flitting fairy of another world,
  Ethereal creature of a sylphic sphere ;
Wilt leave me now with brain so dazed and
    whirled,
  And angelwise, soar off and disappear ?
I will not from my heaven thus be hurled !
  I 'll meet you later and we 'll have a beer.

FANCY A-WING.

IN ITALIA.

GOLD dawn 'twixt Alps and Appenines !
　　Gold dawn on vales and olive trees,
And pent in golden celandines,
　　Blown sweet by winds from southern seas !
Birds chant their matins to the skies,
　　Perched high on old castello walls,
　　And everywhere the sunlight falls
Glad anthems and hosannas rise !

　　　Across the flower-bespangled grass
　　　　She walks amid the peasant throng,
　　　With lifted face to morning mass,
　　　　Outpouring all her soul in song.
　　　White arum-lilies deck her breast,
　　　　And for her vestal's diadem,
　　　Upon her flowing tresses rest
　　　　Some stainless stars of Bethlehem.

Dim clouds of gold and amethyst
　　Across the azure zenith creep,

Beaux and Belles

And vanish in the golden mist,
   Like white feluccas on the deep.
High noon 'twixt purple peaks and sea,
   And silence, save for cooing doves,
   As lovely as the painted Loves
Of Orpheus and Eurydice.

She lingers in the scented shades
   To eat her figs and drink her milk,
The fairest of the Tuscan maids,
   With dreaming eyes and hair of silk,
With lips as red as tulip-bells
   Amidst the maize in time of May,
And fragrant as the asphodels
   That bloom where Dante sleeps for
   aye.

The vesper chimes have ceased to ring,
   The gold has changed to silver light,
And Philomel begins to sing
   Gay ritornellos to the night ;
In vine-hung ways are heard guitars,
   And youthful laughter, low and sweet,
   And love-words, never obsolete,
Low-murmured to the witness stars.

Fancy A-Wing

Beneath the silvered lichen leaves
She lifts her lips for his caress,
With love that dies not, nor deceives,
And knows no law but happiness ;
'Twas love like this that Sappho sung
On Lesbian hills long, long ago,
And that, when Italy's art was young,
Was known to Michael Angelo !

AHOLABEH.

WHERE cool Rohini's waters flow
    From haunts in Himalayan shades
To Gunga's sacred tide below,
    Through gardens and resplendent glades,
Wherein gay sunbirds whirr and swing
From flower to flower on tireless wing,
And golden orioles tilt and sing
    Of love through all the day,—
The Sâkya Rose is blossoming,
        Aholabeh !

Aholabeh ! a hope attained !
    A rose-white Princess passing fair ;
Her small, soft hands are henna-stained,
    A garland binds her scented hair ;
Her soorma-lustred lashes seek
To veil the love that burns her cheek,`
The love too great for lips to speak,
    And strong to live alway ;

Fancy A-Wing

For kissing them thy gods grow weak,
    Aholabeh !

Tall Prince, whose kriss is keen to kill
  The tiger crouched in kusa-grass,
Not Krishna thou, to have thy will
  At sylvan sport with her, and pass ;
No gift of fruits or frankincense,
Of champak, musk, or ornaments
Of nakre or of gold, contents,
  But faith of thee for aye ;
All pride in meek magnificence,
    Aholabeh !

Then build thy house of ganthi-flowers,
  Set stolen stars against their blue,
Build heaven for her in earthly bowers,
  And sheathe thy sword if thou wouldst woo.
Lo, in the garden of her sire
She waits for thee in bride's attire,
With downcast eyes and lips of fire,
  The Light of Himalay,
The soul of all the world's desire,
    Aholabeh !

IN THE HIGHLANDS.

THE sweet Loch Lomond finds a bed
   Within the Highlands' warm embrace ;
Ben Lomond lifts his tawny head
   To kiss the harvest moon's fair face ;
The flowering fields look up in love
To all the amorous stars above.

   Oh, pluck some purple ling for me,
   And one white daisy bring for me,
   And sing for me, and sing for me,
     " Glenogie " and " Prince Charlie ! "

A perfect peace lies on the moor,
   The tender myrtle drapes the dune,
And Philomel's sweet overture
   Has set the banks and braes in tune ;
All Scotland is a bonnie bride,
Whose dreamful sighs her joys confide.

   How gude to hear the skirl o' pipes
   O'er bracken, burn, and barley,

Fancy A-Wing

When Donald plays and Janet sings
"Glenogie" and "Prince Charlie!"

By limpid lake half hid from light,
  Embowered by the heather blooms,
My Highland lassie sits to-night
  And quaffs with me the night's perfumes,
Her soul and mine in harmony
With all we hear and all we see.

" Threescore o' nobles rode up the king's ha',
But bonnie Glenogie's the pride o' them a',
Wi' his milk-white steed and his bonnie black
    e'e ;
Glenogie, dear mither, Glenogie for me ! "

With eyes more soft than eyes of dove,
  And breath more sweet than whin or thyme,
She lifts her lips in languid love,
  And with my lips constructs a rhyme ;—
How wondrous is a wistful word
With earth and sky in rapt accord !

" I'll to Lochiel, and Appin, and kneel to
    them,
  Down by Lord Murray and Roy of Kil-
    darlie :

Brave Mackintosh, he shall fly to the field wi'
    them,—
    These are the lads I can trust wi' my
       Charlie !"

Ah, ne'er shall wane this harvest moon,
    This night of nights shall last for aye,
And though I know a Spain's hot noon,
    Or in the Northland have my day,
Ben Lomond still will tower above,
My lassie kiss my lips in love.

" *Down thro' the Lowlands, down wi' the*
    Whigamore,
    Loyal true Highlanders, down wi' them
      rarely!
Ronald and Donald, drive on wi' the broad
    claymore
    Over the necks o' the foes o' Prince Charlie !
Follow thee! follow thee! wha wadna follow
    thee,
    King o' the Highland hearts, bonnie Prince
      Charlie !"

THE HOMESICK WANDERER.

OH, for a breath of bracken and heather,
  As up from the south the spring comes
    by !
Oh, for a walk in the glad warm weather,
  Under the blue of Scotland's sky !
Oh, for the sound of the laughing waters,
  Kissing the Highlands' crags of gray,
And a sight of the fairest of Scotia's
    daughters—
  The lass that loved me in Colonsay !

  " Fhir a bhata ! Fhir a bhata ! "
I can hear the boatmen singing,
In my ears the pipes are ringing,
  " Fhir a bhata ! Fare thee well ! "

Oh, to live over the olden story,
  Told of bonnie and braw McPhail,
Who left the Isle for the fields of glory,
  Bearing the ruby that would not pale,

Would not change till she that waited
  Proved untrue and drifted away,
And joy was theirs when the two were mated,
  And he was the hero of Colonsay !

  " Fhir a bhata ! Fhir a bhata ! "
'T was the last sweet sound, I mind me,
Heard as Ulva paled behind me,—
  " Fhir a bhata ! Fare thee well ! "

How would it be with the nameless rover,
  After his years on the barren main ?
Never may *he* live the old tale over,—
  All his battles have been in vain ;
Sadly my eyes in the moonlight glisten,
  Heavy my heart through the weary day,
As ever and ever I seem to listen
  To voices behind me in Colonsay.

  " Fhir a bhata ! Fhir a bhata ! "—
And that sound of boatmen singing
In my ears will e'er be ringing,—
  " Fhir a bhata ! Fare thee well ! "

HAFIZ.

I.

WHEN Hafiz sang in Samarcand,
　　Through tender twilights, sweet with
　　　　balm,
Trooped star-eyed youths and maids to hear,
　　And woo 'neath citron-tree and palm ;
The nightingales were awed and mute ;
　　Peace brooded over all the skies ;
And sweeter than a magic lute
　　His glad notes rang, or broke in sighs.
The spell of love was on the land
When Hafiz sang in Samarcand.

II.

Where Hafiz sleeps by bastioned walls
　　The poppies set the fields in flame ;
White asphodels above his breast
　　Speak silently his sacred name ;

In rose-wreathed bowers rough songs are
   heard,
  And ribald laughter over wine,;
A ruffian slays, for one mad word,
  His rival at a wanton's shrine.
Then in the dusk sad silence falls
Where Hafiz sleeps by bastioned walls.

CHRYSANTHEMUM.

CHRYSANTHEMUMS! In dear old
    days
  When I was such a happy man,
And wandered in the pleasant ways,
  I once sojourned in far Japan ;
Where Ti Tum, of the satin eyes
  And luring grace, each morn would come
To bring me (ah ! the sweet surprise !)
  A Japanese chrysanthemum !

My *musmee* knew my every wish ;
  How charmingly she served me tea,
With her own picture on the dish,—
  Less sweet and dainty, though, than she ;
And when I gave a kiss for this
  In token of reward, Ti Tum
Gave me another soon—that is,
  A Japanese chrysanthemum !

We lounged for long in fields of flowers,
  We sat together in the shade ;

Beaux and Belles

I ne'er have known such happy hours
  As those for me my *musmee* made.
'T was an ideal life to lead !—
  Of all delights the very sum !
And she was fair—herself, indeed,
  A Japanese chrysanthemum !

And when the dreamer ceased to dream,
  And all his idols turned to clay,
No after joys could e'er redeem
  The hours his *musmee* laughed away.
And did I leave her in Japan ?
  And did she not my own become ?
I have her still—upon a fan !—
  My Japanese chrysanthemum !

So you may wear the flower you choose,
  The pink or pansy, rue or rose,
But pardon if I 've different views,
  In memory I this one chose ;
Not for its fragance do I care,
  'T is not so beautiful as some,
But I am quite content to wear
  A Japanese chrysanthemum !

DARK as the dawn on the still, wide water,
　　When the fog and the mist hang low,
Was the face of the Southland's beautiful
　　　daughter,
　　Little Felicia of Mexico ;
Aye, as the languorous dusks and olden
　　Over the Guadalquiver's tide,
But bright her eyes as the starlight golden
　　The night in the Southland glorified.

Sweet as the breath of the myosotis,
　　Little Felicia's lips, and red ;
Born was she of love and the lotus,
　　Deep in June in a peri's bed.
Stole from the Sun his warmth and languor,
　　Stole from the flowers their beauty and
　　　sweet,
Leavened her love with a spirit of anger,
　　Learned of a cougar that played at her
　　　feet.

Beaux and Belles

Little Felicia—the saints befriend her !—
  Lost her heart in an evil hour,
Loved with a love that was true and tender,
  And joy was all of her bridal dower.
Where was the Sun with protecting favor?
  Where was the cougar with deadly claws?
Ay de mi ! there was none to save her,—
  Well had she died in the cougar's jaws !

Down by the sea where the soft warm water
  Kisses the banks with murmurous sighs,
Perished the Southland's beautiful daughter,
  Canopied only by peaceful skies ;
But ah ! not alone, for lo ! beside her
  He who had wooed her and wrought her
    woe
Lay dead from the sting of the Spanish
    spider,—
  Little Felicia of Mexico !

VARIA

123

I DO not sing the martyred brave,
  Who dared and died for liberty,
Nor those who breasted wind and wave
  To win a world across the sea ;
Nor yet the knights of olden days,
  Whose name and fame were England's
    pride,
Whose valor poets vied to praise,
  And every victory glorified.

I do not sing the fair and fond,
  Whose charms both king and slave have
    sung,
Whose sceptre, Love, since being dawned,
  Has swayed the hearts of old and young ;
Nor is my lyre attuned to laud
  The worth of wealth, or wit, or wine,
Which shallow sonneteers applaud
  At ten or twenty cents a line.

Beaux and Belles

I do not sing of snow nor spring,
 Of flowery fields, nor moonlit glades,
Of birds that whirl on tireless wing
  Through all the summer's lights and
   shades ;
Of none of these ; they 're out of date ;
 I 've laid them all upon the shelf ;
My theme is one of greater weight—
 I sing of nothing but Myself !

TO EMMA EAMES.

THOU conquerest all our hearts, and then
  Bidst us adieu for larger spheres;
We can but say: "*Auf wiedersehen*,
  Come back to us in future years!"

Auf wiedersehen! But ere the sea
  Has borne thee from us for long days,
A farewell gift I bring to thee—
  A simple wreath of honest praise.

No frankincense, or myrrh, or gold,
  No songs like the immortal Keats';
But flowers that you may kiss and hold—
  A wreath of tender marguerites.

How often, in a careless hour,
  I've looked at lilies, musingly,
And thought: "Had lilies voice of power,
  How wondrous sweet that voice would
    be!"

And when I heard thee, flower of youth,
  With all thy sweetness, grace, and art,
Lo ! 't was the lily's voice, in truth,
  And still it echoes in my heart.

I place my garland at thy feet—
  A grateful gift—with eyes still wet
With tears for gentle *Marguerite*,
  For *Elsa* and for *Juliette* !

May, 1892.

'T IS no design of mine, God wot,
    That I should be forever " broke,"
But there 's a time I envy not
    The best that comes to wealthy folk ;
'T is when, at Mistress Polly's board—
    You know the house, 10, Arcady—
I share with other guests her hoard
    Of bread, and cheese, and beer—and glee.

We gather there on Sunday nights,
    A jolly crowd of eight or nine,
And all have healthy appetites,
    Since most of us forget to dine.
Then what a feast awaits our eyes !
    There 's everything the heart can wish ;
The world is just the shape and size
    Of Mistress Polly's chafing dish !

I never yet have understood
    The source of Mistress Polly's art,

Beaux and Belles

And why her rarebits are so good
   They never fail to reach the heart.
I 've supped at times—say once or twice—
   With big-bugs at Delmonico's,
But things have never tasted nice—
   Just why, Magician Polly knows.

Come round some time to No. 10,
   And be bohemian—what say?
You 'll find no place that 's better when
   You want to drive dull care away.
Bring all your jokes and funny things
   To add to Mistress Polly's cheer ;
We 'll have a banquet fit for kings
   Of toasted bread, and cheese, and beer !

A PREDICAMENT.

SHE is very dear to me,
    She is all the world, I ween,
What think you her name may be ?—
    Josephine !

You would guess it by her looks,
    You would know it by her air,
She is like the girls in books—
    Very fair !

You cannot resist surprise
    When you 're told this fairy queen
Has the sweetest hazel eyes
    Ever seen !

And you will rejoice to know
    That her cheeks were made to bite,
That her skin is like the snow,
    Soft and white.

And her lips are full and red,
    Like the berries of the mead ;

Beaux and Belles

" None but you I 'll kiss," she said,
    " No, indeed ! "

But this witch is full of guile,
    For she added, not in fun,
" Even you must wait awhile,
    Till we 're one ! "

Did the like you ever hear
    Since your great-grandmamma's day,
When all girls were prudes, I fear ?—
    Did you, say ?

Tell me, please, what I 'm to do,
    To my prayers she will not hark ;
Shall I die and go straight to—— ?
    (Question mark !)

Ah, there 's little hope for me,
    So why rail at unkind fate?
Maybe your advice would be,—
    Simply wait!

But I cannot well comply,
    So she never can be mine,
For she 's only six, and I—
    Sixty-nine !

NOCTURNE.

MOONLIGHT, and the madness thereof,
    and the love ;
Moonlight and peace below, and moonlight
    and peace above ;
The trees have sighed and are silent, the seas
    have sunk into sleep,
And who that looks in the sky's fair face
    could think that the sky could weep ?

"I LOVE YOU."

HOW many fleet, sweet years have passed
    Since that glad hour she deigned to say—
Hath time been slow, hath time been fast?
    Men live a lifetime in a day.
I still can feel her hand in mine,
    Her warm caress in swift delight,—
How many years?   Hath time no sign?
    Or did it all occur last night?

Last night ! It seems a faint, sweet dream !
    Last night !   And I have not grown gray
I feel the thrill, the joy supreme
    I knew when first I heard her say—
Cold—is it cold?   I did not know ;
    I thought the blast a tender tune,
I saw the falling flakes of snow,
But thought them blossoms of the June.

Stand closer, for mine eyes grow dim,
    Perhaps, who knows ? the end is near ;

Varia

I wonder if she thinks of him
  Her three words gave a life-time's cheer.
Last night ! I hear the music yet,
  I kiss her lips, I hear her say—
God, tell me, does a soul forget
  When it goes forth to endless day ?

THE SCRIBE'S SWEETHEART.

O FLATTERING tongue of fair Susanne !
　　She calls my poems " pipes of Pan,"
She laughs at all my jokes, and sees
In each some wondrous qualities ;
To her my stories are the best
With which the world was ever blest ;
My books, she says, should all be found
In every house above the ground ;
In short, I 'm Byron, Tennyson,
And Swift and Shakespeare all in one !

Ah, flattering tongue of fair Susanne !
If she were but the editor man !

FAIRY TALES.

" ONCE on a time ! " O magic phrase,
　　That brought the light to eager eyes
In careless childhood's golden days,
　　When we were happy and unwise !
When gnomes and giants, sylphs and sprites,
　　Abode in towers and forests grand,
In that old realm of youth's delights,
　　The wondrous realm of Fairy-land !

Then Princes dressed in cloth of gold,
　　And Princesses were strangely fair ;
To castles gloomy, weird and old,
　　Oafs dragged their captives by the hair ;
Queens rode on palfreys that had wings ;
　　Knights went to war in ten-league shoes,
And half the men on earth were Kings,—
　　The other half formed Retinues !

Oh, Fancy-land of happy youth !
　　Thy joys, alas, are all too fleet ;

Beaux and Belles

By years so fraught with cruel truth
   Our disillusion is complete.
But even yet, how strange and dear
   The wonders of that golden clime,
And how our pulses thrill to hear
   Those luring words, " Once on a time ! "

FUTILE INTUITION.

" NIGHT has a myriad eyes,"
    So runs the legend old,
But Love has a myriad more, I hold—
And still Love is not wise.

A MESSAGE.

IT is too much to ask you to forgive,
  For bitter silence, like rank weeds, has
    grown
Between us for so long, that though I live
  A hundred years I cannot half atone,
Nor by the magic of regretful deeds
Change into flowers of trust the bitter weeds.

But could you for a little space forget
  All that has happened wrong, and live
    again
Those happy hours when one pale violet
  Of all you brought me to my bed of pain,
Was more to me than favor of a king,
Because your love spake in the little thing ;

And mount with me once more those creak-
    ing stairs
  To that high room where all the old books
    lay,

Varia

Where, all forgetful of the world and its
   affairs,
  Our love found speech upon that perfect
    day,
And where, like Romola and Tito, first
Our lips assuaged each other's burning
    thirst ;—

Could you forget, I say, but for a space,
  The after-wrongs that tore us far apart,
I think the old sweet love would light your
    face,
  And there would be a glad song in your
    heart ;
And if you knew how deeply I regret,
You were not you, unless you did forget.

A WOMAN'S LOVE.

'TIS you that have brought me sorrow,
  And stained my life with tears,
That have made to-day and to-morrow
  As dreary and long as years ;
You are false to the faith we plighted,
  And swore by the stars above,
And the wrong cannot be righted—
  But this is the pay of love !

Yet I am only a woman,
  To love while ever I live,
And be it divine or human,
  Should find it joy to forgive ;
One rapturous hope I cherish
  In all my grief and unrest,
That ere I shall fail and perish,
  You will clasp me again to your breast !

OH, well for the joy,—
It is sweet ! It is sweet !
The sin is in bud,
Its heart in retreat.

Alack for the joy !
For time will disclose
The shame of the sin,
As the heart of the rose.

RECONCILIATION.

CLASP hands, if ye love, and listen,
　　Clasp hands, and look into my eyes,
O'er few are the years to kiss in,
　　And I take it that ye are wise ;
True love is a radiant jewel,
　　But its splendor will pale and pass,
And the dark of the night is cruel,
　　And there is no balm in "alas !"

Then oh, while the dews of morning,
　　The morning of love and of life,
Are still on your lips, take warning,
　　And waste no moment in strife ;
Clasp hands, and kiss, and banish
　　The evil from mind and heart,
Kiss now, ere your passions vanish,
　　And leave you dead and apart !

TOO NATURAL.

HER cheeks are roses red and white,
   Her mouth a cleft red rose,—
But ah, she is too natural quite—
   Her tongue 's a thorn, he knows !

THE POET'S FAREWELL.

THEY say my muse has flown for aye,
　　And that my poet's day is done,
　That I am but a "sinking sun,"
Who sang so sweetly yesterday.

My masters know . . . Yea, it is o'er,
　　With broken heart I close the book,
　Put by my pen with one last look,
And turn away to dream no more.

What now, beloved, remains unsaid?
　　One wish, perhaps, before the end—
　That you will think of me as *friend*,
And call me fair when I am dead.

A FLING AT POETS.

IF I had a girl with golden hair,
   And teeth of exquisite pearl,
And eyes that were gems, resplendent, rare,
   Do you know what I 'd do with that girl ?

I 'd carry the beautiful, precious thing
   Right down to a jeweler's place,
And I 'd sell her quick for what she would
      bring
   As an ornament to her race.

PLAINT OF A POET.

IN good old times the Poet's lot
    Was one of honor, pride, and praise,
And poesy was not a blot
    On one's fair name, as nowadays ;
Alas ! this unregenerate age
    Has no respect for Homer's art,
And deems all Poets need a cage,
    Or dwelling-place from men apart.

An inoffensive chap am I,
    Who have my hair cut now and then,
And dash off things about the " sky,"
    And " snow," and " Spring has come
        again " ;
And everywhere I chance to go
    By sneers and scoffs I am attacked,
Folks nod at me and whisper low :
    " Oh, he 's a Poet !" meaning " cracked."

Varia

One friend alone has proven true,
  And once I said : "Pray condescend
To tell me how it happens you
  Deign be a modern Poet's friend?"
He grasped my hand. "Because, to wit :
  You 've been maligned in hut and hall ;
I 've read all things you ever writ,
  You 're not a Poet, sir, at all!"

THE END.